ESSENTIAL TIPS

Planning a
SMALL YARD

D0743517

ESSENTIAL TIPS

Planning a
SMALL YARD

CONTRIBUTING EDITOR
John Brookes

A DK PUBLISHING BOOK

Editor Damien Moore
Art Editor Alyson Kyles
DTP Designer Mark Bracey
Series Editor Charlotte Davies
Series Art Editor Clive Hayball
Production Controller Lauren Britton
US Editor Laaren Brown

First published in Canada in 1996 by
Fenn Publishing Ltd.
1090 Lorimar Drive, Mississiauga, Ontario, Canada, L5S 1R8

ISBN 1-55168-056-4

Text film output by The Right Type, Great Britain
Reproduced by Colourscan, Singapore
Printed and bound by Graphicom, Italy

E S S E N T I A L TIPS

CONSIDERING SURFACES

PLANNING YOUR PLANTING

PLANTING ENVIRONMENTS

BASIC DESIGN CONSIDERATIONS

1 MAKING THE MOST OF YOUR SPACE

To realize the potential of a small space you must first abandon your preconceptions about the nature of a "yard" – the word often evokes visions of lawns and flowerbeds. Traditional planting is, however, only one of the options open to you.

Any outdoor space, be it a rooftop, a basement site, or a window ledge, can be treated as a "yard" in that, with a little careful planning and a practical design, the most neglected space can be converted into an attractive extension of your home.

△ SUSPENDED SPLENDOR
A hanging basket provides a versatile option for small-scale gardening. Here, the geraniums and verbenas ensure long-term color.

△ VERTICAL PLANTING
A bare wall is transformed by a spectacular display of climbing and trailing plants.

◁ CONTAINER GARDENING
Use containers to introduce color and fragrance into awkward spots such as rooftops or subground sites, which are impossible to garden traditionally.

2 AN OUTDOOR ROOM

Think of your outside space as a room where you can eat, entertain guests, or enjoy a moment of solitude away from the pressures of urban living. Although this is easier to imagine in a southern climate, sun alone does not make for a comfortable outdoor space. Consider how you can minimize drafts, create a degree of privacy, disguise unsightly views, and use color and fragrance to create a pleasing ambience.

A GARDEN SANCTUARY

3 FOUR KEY FACTORS

It is worth investing plenty of time at the planning stage of designing your yard. You must try to find a design that satisfies a number of variable factors: the way you wish to use the space, the limitations of the site, the character of the surroundings, and the amount of money available for materials and plants.

4 INSIDE-OUT GARDENING

Make sure that your outdoor space is attractive when viewed from inside. A cramped yard will seem less so if it is a harmonious extension of the interior room that it adjoins.

- Analyze your interior design: is it period or modern? Consider how you can interpret the style outdoors.

- Consider how you can harmonize color in your house and yard.
- If possible, choose a similar type of flooring for your yard space as you have used for your inside space.
- Choose furniture that is suitable for outdoor or indoor use to extend the link between the two spaces.

5 COMPLEMENTARY ELEMENTS

In order to create a coherent and pleasing style in your outside space, you must treat each element of your garden – be it walls, fences, furniture, steps, or plant pots – as part of a single design. Bear in mind how one relates to another in terms of color, shape, and function. A haphazard approach – building a raised bed here, planting a shrub there – and an assortment of poorly considered bits and pieces will result in an unstylish mishmash, and will also make your small space seem even smaller than it actually is. A successful garden, whether it be at ground level or on a balcony or rooftop, is one in which all its elements, from the smallest to the biggest, are in accord.

◁ GOTHIC-STYLE YARD
This individual creation may not be to everyone's taste, but it is certainly a bold design that makes a visually positive and coherent statement.

▽ GOTHIC SEAT
Pots and furnishings should complement the overall design.

6 FIND YOUR OWN STYLE

Plan your own yard to satisfy yourself and your family and not necessarily other people. Copying of another design completely may result in disappointment. It is, of course, a good idea to study other people's designs (and styles from various cultures) as sources of inspiration. Ultimately you must seek to evolve a style that suits your personality, because your yard like your clothes or your furnishings, should be an expression of your own taste. Adopt a design that suits your lifestyle. For example, you must consider whether you have the time or, indeed, the inclination to nurture plants, or would you prefer a low-maintenance plan?

△ BONSAI BEAUTY
Seek inspiration from the simplicity of an oriental-style design (see p.68).

△ FORMAL GARDEN
Formal garden styles such as this require regular and meticulous maintenance.

▽ PERIOD OR MODERN?
These garden accessories would be suitable only in a modern-style garden.

△ LOW-MAINTENANCE YARD
A yard such as this, where the textures and colors of the structure take precedence over the planting, is suitable if your busy lifestyle leaves little time for gardening.

7 ARCHITECTURAL REFLECTIONS

It is likely that the style of your home has already influenced your choice of interior decorations and furnishings. Let it do the same for your yard. Each architectural style has facets that can be reflected in the line and form of the yard's layout, whatever its size.

- Select materials that complement those from which your house is made: stone, brick, or wood.

- Select and arrange containers and furnishings – and even plants – that reflect the style of your house.
- You do not have to be historically accurate in every detail, but try to capture the general mood of a style.

▽ REFLECTIONS IN WINDOWS
Here, flint stone surrounding a young fig tree echoes the materials used in the walls of the house. The mass of planting reflects the rural style of the building.

SPECIFIC SITES

8 WINDOWS

Choose plants and containers that suit the style of your window by looking at the color of the window frame and its surroundings.
- If you have no windowsill or your window opens outward, hang pots beneath your window or grow a climber from ground level and train it around the frame.

DELICATE DISPLAY ▷
A grapevine, Vitis, *and a window box planted with delicate geraniums decorate this simple window and its rustic border.*

9 BALCONIES

Balconies are often buffeted by strong winds, so select plants that will thrive in exposed conditions (*see p.51*). Grow less-hardy species in the shelter of the hardier plants. Train climbers like ivy up a secure trellis to give shelter and a measure of privacy, or to obscure an ugly view. Make sure you fasten any containers and furnishings so that they do not present a danger to your neighbors below.

◁ HEAVYWEIGHT CONTAINERS
Pots of plants, especially when wet, can be very heavy. Consult a structural engineer about the weight capacity of your balcony.

10 CREATING A ROOFTOP RETREAT

As much as possible, treat your roof space as you would an indoor space, so that you create a roomlike atmosphere. Weatherproof flooring or lightweight paving will make your space more congenial. Consult a structural engineer to establish the strength of your roof.
▪ It is advisable to choose lightweight pots for plants and to place them close to supporting walls.

▪ Choose and arrange your planting carefully – many species will not tolerate exposure to intense rooftop sunshine and strong wind (see p.51).
▪ Spread a layer of gravel or pebbles over the surface of soil in pots. This will help retain moisture and stop the top surface from blowing away.

LIGHTWEIGHT CONTAINER ▷
A lightweight wooden window box is a practical option for most roof sites.

▽ STURDY SITUATION
This rooftop site is sturdy enough to support a veritable forest of shrubs and trees, including juniper and New Zealand flax in heavy terracotta pots.

11 HOW TO ENHANCE A SUBGROUND SITE

Low subground areas can be gloomy and damp. However, there are many ways of making such areas stylish and pleasant to use.
• Make sure that the foundation is waterproof so that leaks and moisture do not damage the floor.
• Experiment with color to bring interest to a subground area and to brighten it up if it is shady. Consider painting the walls or laying bright or colorful surfacing materials.

• Mirrors can make your site seem larger and increase light for plants.
• Provide a feature, whether a piece of sculpture, a seat, or a plant, to anchor the eye within the site.
• Choose plants that are tolerant of shade (*see p.50*), many of which have interesting foliage shapes.
• Create single-color planting designs in light tones of gold and silver as an effective way of bringing life to a shady basement area.

◁ A MOSSY POT
A water feature anchors the eye within this shady site.

▽ SHADE-LOVING PLANT
This elegant Solomon's-seal, Polygonatum, *with forget-me-nots,* Myosotis, *will thrive in the shade.*

12 HOW TO ENHANCE NARROW SPACES

Build up an internal structure that draws the eye from side to side to create an impression of breadth in a narrow space, and use screens to break up the view down the garden. Screens can also block drafts – a common problem in narrow sites.

Long, narrow spaces draw the eye through them – a disadvantage if the end point is a dilapidated fence. Turn this into a positive quality by placing a dramatic feature, such as a statue, a large urn, or a *trompe l'oeil*, at the back of the garden.

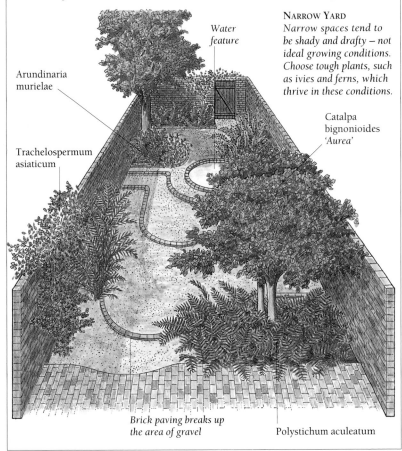

NARROW YARD
Narrow spaces tend to be shady and drafty – not ideal growing conditions. Choose tough plants, such as ivies and ferns, which thrive in these conditions.

Water feature

Arundinaria murielae

Trachelospermum asiaticum

Catalpa bignonioides 'Aurea'

Brick paving breaks up the area of gravel

Polystichum aculeatum

13 DECORATIVE DOORWAYS

The material you select for surfacing around your doorway, the style and color of your door, its fixtures and fittings, and pots and tubs placed around it should all suit the style of your home and set the mood for what lies within. Choose a light or a pot for the doorway, or hang a wreath on the door to make your entrance welcoming to visitors. But be sure that such items are firmly attached, for weight alone is no deterrent to a determined thief.

◁ COUNTRY-STYLE ENTRANCE
This porch was added to the cottage by its new owners, but it is designed in keeping with the older building.

14 IMAGINATIVE STEPS

Steps afford the frustrated urban gardener valuable space for growing plants (in pots alongside the steps or on the steps themselves).
- Plants alongside steps should have bold, architectural shapes to balance the strong structural form of the steps themselves. Evergreen shrubs are ideal; they give year-round shape and interest to your planting.
- Select climbing plants to decorate handrails and adjacent walls.
- Grow colorful annuals in pots on the steps themselves – but do not obstruct the stairs.

△ LEAVING SPACE FOR THYME
These attractive garden steps have been designed to include planting space for a mat-forming plant such as this thyme.

BOUNDARY STRUCTURES

15 WALLED YARDS

In urban areas, small yards are often hemmed in by the walls of neighboring gardens or buildings. The effect is often constricting, but the following measures can help:

- Grow climbing plants to bring life and color to unsightly walls.

- Use retaining walls within your garden to add interest and to lead the eye from the top of the boundary wall down to ground level.
- Include bold internal features, such as a mass of planting or a statue, to hold the eye within the site.

△ A RURAL SETTING
This stone wall, an attractive feature in itself, also provides a splendid background for this elegant, winding wisteria.

16 DECORATING WALLS

Don't be afraid to decorate outside walls in a similar manner to the walls in your house.

- Painting walls will liven up a small, enclosed space and counteract its oppressiveness.
- Attach shelves to your walls to support pots and curiosities such as exotic shells and pebbles.
- Decorate exterior walls with sculptural panels, statues, and tiles, just as you would indoors.
- Use trelliswork to disguise unsightly walls.

△ WALL WINDER
Clematis is a very popular twining plant, renowned for its long flowering period.

▽ A SOFT OPTION
A mass of planting softens the hard line of the wall.

△ FERNS & FLOWERS
Here, a courtyard wall is decorated with trelliswork hung with an array of pots and plants, including many ferns that thrive in shade.

◁ CERAMIC SUNSHINE
A ceramic sun creates a simple and charming focal point on an outdoor wall.

17 WALL FLOWERS

In yards where ground space is limited, climbing plants are invaluable and they bring an effective vertical element to any garden design.

- Evergreen climbers, such as the passionflower (*Passiflora caerulea*) shown below, are especially useful because they provide a strong structural element in the garden all year.
- Clothing a wall with a combination of climbers can bring continual interest. Clematis and vines are especially happy to grow through other plants.
- If you do not have a suitable wall or fence on which to grow climbing plants, you can make or purchase a freestanding support, trellis, or stake.

◁ PASSIONFLOWER

FAVORITE CLIMBERS
Actinidia chinensis
Akebia quinata
Berberidopsis corallina
Campsis grandiflora
Clematis alpina
Clematis montana
Clianthus puniceus
Hedera colchica
Hedera helix 'Hibernica'
Humulus lupulus
Ipomoea hederacea
Jasminum mesnyi
Jasminum officinale
Lonicera japonica
Lonicera periclymenum
Passiflora caerulea
Polygonum baldschuanicum
Vitis coignetiae
Vitis vinifera
Wisteria sinensis

△ TRAINING SHRUBS
Some shrubs, such as this evergreen Ceanothus, *can be trained to climb up walls.*

◁ CLIMBING ROSES
This brick and stone wall is a handsome feature in its own right. It is an ideal spot for the elegant climbing rose in this unruly, country-style garden.

18 MATERIALS FOR WALLS

When choosing material for a wall, consider how the color and texture will complement your house and its surrounding structural elements.

■ Always take into consideration the unit size of different materials.

■ Visualize the massed effect of a unit – it can be startlingly different from looking at a unit in isolation.

■ Brick is the most popular material for building walls. The enormous range available means that there is a brick to suit almost any setting.

■ In rural locations, local stone will probably best suit the landscape; in urban areas, concrete is often better.

△ MIXED MATERIALS
Using a combination of building materials can be highly effective. This striking wall was constructed with a mixture of brick and flint – ideal for this country garden.

◁ CONCRETE BRICK
These small-scale rock-faced concrete blocks are designed to imitate the effect of traditional clay bricks.

△ PRECAST BLOCKS
These sandstone-colored concrete blocks contain a medium-textured aggregate.

MOTTLED BRICKS △
With a rough-hewn appearance, these engineering bricks are the hardest of all traditional bricks.

△ GEOMETRIC PATTERNS
Although much maligned, this modern type of concrete block is relatively cheap and easier to erect than traditional brick.

NATURAL STONES ▷
Drystone walls are lovely features. The crevices between the stones are ideal for a rock garden.

NATURAL
LIMESTONE

NATURAL
SANDSTONE

19 FENCING FOR YOUR BOUNDARIES

Fencing is a highly versatile and relatively inexpensive material for marking the boundaries of your site. Fences are easier to erect than walls and make good backdrops for planting, but they require more maintenance. The fact that fences provide almost instant privacy gives them an advantage over hedging.

- Use high panels of solid fencing to create a wall-like barrier that is relatively easy to erect. Remember, however, that this type of boundary can make your small site feel even smaller and rather claustrophobic.
- See-through fencing at any height makes a small space seem larger and is an ideal host for climbing plants.

△ TRADITIONAL PICKET FENCING
This garden is enclosed by a traditional white picket fence, which complements the cottage's attractive whitewashed walls.

△ PLANTING THROUGH FENCING
Shrub roses and rock roses have been planted alongside this old, weathered fence to create a traditional rustic feel.

20 BORROW YOUR NEIGHBOR'S YARD

When you are dividing your small plot of land from that of your neighbors, consider the advantage of visually sharing the space. Even a small panel of open fencing will help counteract the boxed-in feeling that can be created by solid fencing.

Open-style fencing will enable you to enjoy the plants growing on your neighbor's side of the fence as well as your own. But bear in mind the possibility that if your neighbor's yard is neglected you may inherit invasive weeds and an eyesore.

21 CHOOSING BOUNDARY FENCING

As with other structural features, care must be taken when selecting a fence to complement the style of your house. You must also consider practical matters, such as the privacy and shelter afforded.

- Wood is the most popular material for fences, and there is a style of lumber fencing to suit almost any purpose and every location.

- It is generally not economical to invest in too cheap a fence. Inferior material will deteriorate rapidly.
- Remember that wood rots if left in direct contact with the ground, so verticals should be placed in a metal shoe and set in concrete.
- Metal and plastic make good alternative fencing materials, needing less care than wood.

RUSTIC WEAVES ▷
Country-style woven and latticework fences can be extremely attractive in the right location. However, the lifespan of such fences is limited.

WOVEN WILLOW ▷

WOVEN HAZEL ▷

RUSTIC LATTICE ▷

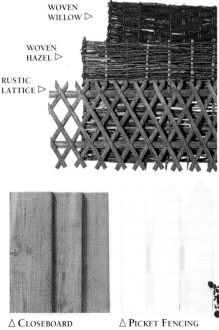

△ PANEL FENCING
This type of fencing is composed of horizontal softwood slats. Allowing maximum privacy, it is ideal for urban areas.

△ BAMBOO
Bamboo stakes, which are an ideal choice for an oriental-style garden (see p.68), can be bound together to make a solid or openwork fence.

△ CLOSEBOARD
This type of fencing is constructed by nailing featheredged verticals to horizontal rails.

△ PICKET FENCING
Highly decorative, picket fencing allows passersby enjoyment of your garden.

22 HEDGES

Consider using hedging as an attractive alternative to a boundary wall or fence. Hedging provides a dramatic backdrop for planting and can also make a strong and colorful feature in its own right. However, since hedging absorbs nutrients out of the soil, it may not be a good choice if your borders are narrow or your soil is particularly dry.

SETTING THE STAGE ▷
This neatly trimmed yew hedge makes a tall, dramatic backdrop for a stunning mass of purple lavender.

23 CHOOSING A BOUNDARY HEDGE

When selecting a hedge, first consider what its function will be. If your first priority is privacy, then an evergreen hedge, such as yew or boxwood, which does not shed its leaves in winter, is the best choice.

Consider, too, the potential height of your hedge planting. Some of the plants that are selected for hedges grow naturally into forest trees. Plants with berries, such as holly, can make very attractive hedges.

YEW
As an evergreen hedge, Taxus baccata *provides year-round interest.*

BOXWOOD
A dense evergreen, Buxus sempervirens *is ideal for creating a sculptural effect.*

CHERRY LAUREL
Prunus laurocerasus *makes a tall, attractive hedge with its shiny evergreen foliage.*

24 DEFENSIVE GARDENING

Deter prowlers and other unwelcome individuals by planting a boundary hedging of shrubs with spines or thorns, such as barberries, or ones with spiky leaves, such as holly, *Ilex*. These plants are often handsome as well as extremely vicious, so they present the security-conscious householder with a more aesthetically pleasing option than the various manufactured deterrents, such as barbed wire.

△ HOLLY, *ILEX* SP.

BEECH
Fagus sylvatica, *a deciduous species, will naturally grow to over 20 ft (6 m) tall.*

△ **FIRETHORN**
This window is protected by the viciously spiny branches of firethorn, Pyracantha, *which has clusters of white flowers in summer.*

HOLLY, *ILEX AQUIFOLIUM*
'GOLDEN QUEEN'

INTERNAL FEATURES

25 THE IMPORTANCE OF STRUCTURAL STYLE

The structure of your yard can be an exciting feature in its own right, and may well need to be if, as is often the case, its size and location allow little or no room for planting. Even for those with more space, the structure is important, for a mass of plants will become a nondescript mess if it is not contained and offset by a strong permanent structure.

■ The materials used to construct the yard, the way they are arranged, and the style of furnishings (which include pots, sculptural features, and lighting), all mold its character.
■ Besides looking at the practical pros and cons of different materials and structural styles, consider how you can integrate "inherited" (often unwelcome) features into the design.

△ SMALL DETAILS
Minor elements in your garden, such as edging stones, should still integrate with major ones.

◁ FOCAL POINT
A piece of sculpture can act as a visual punctuation mark in a small garden design.

△ PERGOLAS, PLANTS, & POTS
A pergola defines a paved terrace area, which is a perfect place to sit and enjoy the garden or entertain friends. These strong structural elements are balanced by a mass of planting.

26 RETAINING WALLS

Use retaining walls to create raised beds for planting material or to support a paved terrace area.

■ At the correct height, a retaining wall makes excellent casual seating when entertaining friends outdoors.

■ Retaining walls are particularly attractive when trailing plants are chosen to grow over them.

■ If designed carefully, raised flower beds can make garden maintenance practical for the elderly, because they make planting more accessible.

△ RAISED BED
This handsome, formally planted retaining wall is a charming feature in itself against the backdrop of hedging.

27 TRAILING PLANTS

Choose plants with a trailing habit to break up and soften the lines of a retaining wall or any other vertical structure, such as a balcony railing.

■ Nasturtiums, *Tropaeolum*, make particularly attractive trailing plants, with their tumbling form, long-lasting flowers, and shapely leaves.

■ Many less-invasive climbers, such as black-eyed Susan vine (*Thunbergia alata*) are fine trailers.

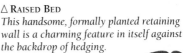

NASTURTIUM

TRAILING PLANT CHOICE
Aubrieta deltoidea
Euonymus fortunei
Genista pilosa
Juniperus
Sanvitalia
Thymus
Verbena

◁ HANGING GARDEN
An annual verbena spills over the edge of a simple wooden trough.

INTERNAL FEATURES

28 SECONDARY FENCING

Consider using fencing within your
yard space as well as around it to create a
roomlike area for entertaining visitors or for
sunbathing – the degree of privacy will
depend on your choice of material (*see p.23*).
▪ Back a yard feature such as a sculpture
with screens made from fencing materials.
▪ Provide support for climbing plants with
openwork or simple stake-and-wire fencing.
▪ Use a wire fence to keep pets away from
your plants without obstructing your view.

△ SIMPLE DIVISION
*Here, sweet pea (Lathyrus
odoratus) is supported by an
improvised fence composed of
twigs linked by string.*

29 DISGUISES FOR EYESORES

Position fencing or screening
material to hide parts of the garden
you would rather are not visible, like
garbage cans, a compost heap, or an
oil tank. Alternatively, planting can
be used to hide unsightly areas, but
this course may require patience.

▪ An openwork fence, such as a trellis,
supporting a climbing plant makes
an attractive screen. But be sure to
choose an evergreen plant or the
eyesore will be exposed each winter.
▪ Evergreen hedging plants such as
boxwood also form effective screens.

△ DISGUISES WITH IVIES
*A drainpipe is partially hidden by a small-
leafed variegated ivy. Climbing plants are
often ideal for softening unsightly walls.*

△ SCREENS & GREENS
*A simple screen conceals a compost heap
in a shady part of the yard. The screen
also serves as a backdrop to potted plants.*

30 CREATING HIDDEN STORAGE SPACE

If possible, try to include a space for storing items like tools and furniture in your garden design. If there is no space for a small shed, build a cupboard space in material that suits the style of your house.

■ Another solution to the problem of storage space in small gardens is to purchase a tool set with a single detachable handle and a range of compatible tool heads – including hoes, rakes, trowels, and cultivators.

△ ATTRACTIVE TRELLIS
A trellis can disguise an unsightly wall – whether it is planted or painted.

31 TRELLISWORK FENCING

Use trellises, available in either square- or diamond-patterned designs, to support climbers on a wall or fence. Freestanding trellises are handy for instant partitions and openwork screening.

■ Trelliswork can be painted or stained and then attached to a wall as a feature in itself (*see p.61*).
■ Extend the height of existing walls without blocking out the light by adding a trellis fence.
■ A glimpse through a trellis will, by blurring the outlines of what lies beyond, give the smallest of spaces the illusion of size.

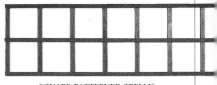

SQUARE-PATTERNED TRELLIS

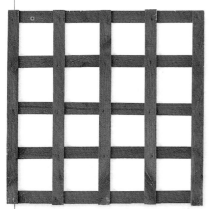

DIAMOND-PATTERNED TRELLIS

△ STURDY TRELLIS
For planting, make sure that your trellis is strong, and attach it with galvanized nails.

32 PERGOLAS

Pergolas have many practical and visual uses in a small yard.

- A pergola can be used to define a roomlike space in semishade for eating and entertaining outdoors.
- It can form a sheltered transition between two separate buildings.
- Use a pergola to reinforce the lines of a path or to direct the eye toward an interesting design feature or view.
- Pergolas can be built from a variety of materials to complement the design of your house and garden.
- Draped in climbing plants, a free-standing pergola can be a stunning feature in its own right.

▽ STRETCHED WIRE
Wire stretched by a turnbuckle forms a taut and discreet pergola horizontal that allows the maximum amount of light to penetrate.

△ WOOD PERGOLA
This attractive timber pergola is supported on one side by brick columns that match the brick patio below.

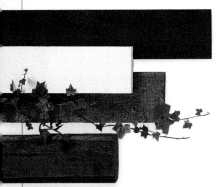

Metal
scaffolding
vertical
supports
painted
horizontal

△ LUMBER SUPPORTS
Wood is the most common material for pergolas. Softwoods are adequate but must be pressure-treated with a preservative.

△ SHAPED, PAINTED SOFTWOOD
These painted horizontals have been cut in decorative shapes. They are supported by scaffolding poles, which are painted white.

33 PLANTS FOR PERGOLAS

Pergolas, whether they are free-standing or adjoining a building, make wonderful hosts to climbing plants. Use plants to soften the overall structure and to provide attractive dappled shade, but bear in mind what the effect will be in winter.

- Plants on pergolas also provide privacy, which can be a great benefit in small urban gardens.
- Remember to consider the weight of planting in relation to the strength of the pergola.

PERFECT FOR PERGOLAS
Actinidia chinensis
Campsis grandiflora
Hedera colchica
Hedera helix 'Hibernica'
Jasminum officinale
Lonicera japonica
Parthenocissus henryana
Polygonum baldschuanicum
Vitis coignetiae
Vitis vinifera
Wisteria

SCENTED ROSES ▷
Fragrant climbing roses can fill a pergola with color and perfume.

◁ VINE
A grapevine (Vitis vinifera) will thrive on a pergola in most situations.

34 POINT OF FOCUS

Strategic focal points in your design will help determine how the eye travels around the garden. The focal point might be a special plant or ornamental tree, but you could also choose a piece of sculpture, a decorative pot, or even a pergola.

- A focal point can lead the eye to an attractive area or distract the eye away from an unsightly feature.
- In a small garden it is often best to use a single, dramatic point of focus.

A STRIKING FOCAL POINT ▷
A simple stone pedestal provides a strong focal point at the end of this path, framed by the hanging racemes of a laburnum.

35 CHOOSING SCULPTURE

Take care when choosing a piece of sculpture or a statue since your choice will have a significant influence on the style and mood of your small yard – adding an elegant finishing touch or an element of humor. Do not, however, be timid with your choice. Generally, the larger the object, the greater the impact it will have. Besides providing a focal point for the garden, it should work from inside the house, too. Place your statue in a commanding position, although not necessarily dominating – you may want your sculpture to counterbalance some other feature.

▽ **A STATUE FOR REFLECTION**
By the waterside, this statue helps to create a contemplative and tranquil atmosphere.

CLASSIC CHOICE ▷
This moss-covered figure, with ivy trained around its base, is ideal for a small formal garden.

36 THE PERFECT POT

The right pot with no planting at all can assume a sculptural quality and demands the same consideration that you would afford to the selection of a piece of sculpture. A classical-style urn, for example, albeit made from reconstituted stone or fiberglass, is grand in style and may not be suited to a location that is humbler in feel. A pot that neither relates to the scale of a space or the overall style can ruin the total effect.

△ SCULPTURAL POT
A classical-style urn can be a feature in itself.

37 ORNAMENTAL TREES

Ornamental trees provide a wonderful element of living sculpture, but be aware of the eventual height of a tree – one that is too large will quickly engulf and unbalance your design. You may want a tree to give shade and shelter (both for yourself and your plants), but consider also that each tree has its own decorative appeal. A magnolia, for example, bears glorious blossoms; and the maple (*Acer palmatum*) displays colorful autumn foliage.

MAGNOLIA △

△ GLORIOUS COLOR
Japanese apricot (Prunus mume) *bears spectacular blossoms in early spring.*

BRIGHT FOLIAGE ▷
Robinia pseudoacacia *'Frisia' is popular for its striking golden foliage.*

38 TIPS FOR TOPIARY

Topiary (training and pruning shrubs to produce bold artificial shapes) can be used to great effect in a small formal garden. In an informal garden, too, a sculptured plant can act as a foil for unruly planting.
- Simple geometric shapes suit small spaces better than figurative designs.
- Where topiary plants are adjacent to buildings, try echoing the shape of an architectural feature, such as an arch.

△ TRAINING IVY ON A FRAME

◁ CLIPPED BOXWOOD SPIRAL

39 FURNITURE FEATURES

In a small yard, it is particularly important that any furniture should be an integral part of your whole design rather than an afterthought.
- Be aware of how the style of your furniture suits that of your yard.
- Consider the impact of the shape and color of your furniture.
- Take as much care positioning your furniture as you would with a mass planting or a piece of sculpture.

△ FOCAL POINT
A path leads the eye as well as the feet to this eye-catching piece of furniture, helping to make it into a sculptural feature in itself.

◁ ELEGANT IRON
This elegant but weathered wrought-iron seat would be an ideal piece of furniture for a country-style garden (see p.64).

40 WATER FEATURES

When used artistically, even a small area of water is always eye-catching, even mesmerizing, when sunlight plays on its still surface.
- The sound of water trickling or flowing gently can be relaxing and can help neutralize urban noise.
- Even where there is little ground space, water can be included in the garden in the form of a wall spout.
- As a general rule, the simpler the use of water in a small garden, the more effective it will be.

SIMPLE WATER FEATURE

41 PLANTING IN & AROUND WATER

Even the most humble water feature can be enhanced by suitable planting both in and around it. Do not, however, attempt to re-create a natural pond look in a small yard, for this leads to a contrived and selfconscious appearance. The smaller the quantity of water, the more restrained both the number and variety of plants should be. Use the vertical stems of irises to contrast with the horizontal line of the water surface or to counterbalance water pouring from a spout.

WATER PLANTS
Aponogeton distachyos
Eichhornia crassipes
Hydrocharis morsus-ranae
Nymphaea "Candidissima"
Nymphoides peltata

MARGINAL PLANTS
Hemerocallis
Hosta
Iris kaempferi
Lysichiton americanum
Peltiphyllum peltatum
Primula florindae

△ BOG ARUM
Lysichiton americanum
a marginal water plant.

WATER LILY ▷
Nymphaea 'Escarboucle',
a floating plant.

42 PLANNING A SMALL ROCK GARDEN

Rock gardens make lovely features, but be sure to make your garden as authentic as possible – an imitation of an alpine rock outcrop as opposed to a pile of discarded rubble in a builder's yard. Select natural rock rather than concrete, and take care to keep any natural veins and crevices flowing in the same direction. Alpine plants, such as gentians and spring crocus, are adapted for specialized climatic conditions and so require excellent drainage and bright light to thrive. If your soil is heavy, dig out the proposed site of your rock garden and replace the soil with a layer of rubble, stone, or ash.

△ ROCK PLANTING
Aubreita *and saxifrage will thrive in a well-prepared rock garden.*

EXPOSED SITES ▷
Heathers, grasses, and low-growing rock plants are ideal for exposed sites.

43 SWIMMING POOLS & HOT TUBS

A lap pool – designed for the sole purpose of swimming laps – need not be more than 10 ft (3 m) in width, but should be no shorter than 8 yds (7 m) long. It is possible to fit a lap pool in a small yard, but little room will be left for anything else. A stationary-swim pool is a smaller alternative. Equipped with a wave machine, it can provide a force of water to swim against. If exercise is not a priority, hot tubs are smaller still. Whatever design you choose, you must cover an outdoor heated pool to conserve energy, so keep the shape simple.

44 PLAY AREAS

With a little effort, a yard can be made into a child's paradise:

Sandbox and nearby slide

- Children enjoy tending their own gardens, so leave a small plot for your child to plant quick-growing annuals, such as sunflowers, with suitable child-size tools.
- Trees may be able to support a simple swing or just a tire tied to a length of rope.
- When building a play area, keep in mind an alternative use for later years. A raised sandbox, for instance, could be turned into a pond.
- Avoid plants with thorns or poisonous berries.

A CHILD'S PARADISE ▷
This garden, designed with children in mind, has been planted with species that attract butterflies, such as Buddleia.

TRADITIONAL BIRDBATH

45 ATTRACTING BIRDS

Stone birdbaths (traditional features in many formal and cottage-style gardens) can provide a delightful focal point in a small garden, regardless of whether you are interested in attracting wildlife. If you *are* an avid bird-watcher, consider growing plants that attract birds. Where space permits, an apple tree is possibly the best choice. It supports a host of insects, which birds will feed on; its blossoms are enjoyed by bullfinches; and a wide variety of birds will be enticed by its fruit. However small your yard, there will always be space for a simple birdhouse, nesting box, or feeder.

37

CONSIDERING SURFACES

46 SUITABLE SURFACES

GRAVEL & TILE

The surface material you choose for your outside space should suit your garden as much as the flooring inside your home suits its various rooms. Give serious consideration to the color, style, cost, and practical suitability of the various options that are available to you. Materials can be successfully mixed, but always keep in mind the final result that you want to achieve.

47 HARD OR SOFT SURFACES?

Hard surfaces such as stone and concrete provide ideal floors for furniture, statues, pots, and other features. They require minimal maintenance, and hard paving can be a feature in its own right.

Gravel and other soft materials are perfect for locations where little will grow and where paving is not practical, such as beneath a tree. The best solution is often a balance of both hard and soft surfacing that creates interesting textural patterns.

COBBLESTONES ▷
An attractive traditional material, cobbles are not the most comfortable of surfaces to walk on.

◁ GRAVEL & WOODCHIPS
Soft surfaces come in a huge variety of textures and colors and are easy to lay in awkward areas.

48 PAVING PATTERNS

Small pavers are ideal for creating surface patterns. Traditional brick pavers can be used to create a variety of different effects. Set them in a basket-weave pattern, for example, to create a cottagelike, country flavor; interlocking boxes create a strong graphic effect; and a herringbone pattern gives a more random informal look.

BASKET WEAVE   **INTERLOCKING**   **HERRINGBONE**

△ **RADIAL DESIGN**
Small unit paving has been used in this garden to create an interesting radial design that is softened by planting.

49 PAVING CHOICE

When selecting paving, opt for a color to blend with your house. Make sure that you wet a sample before you buy, to check the color change. The color of paving can change in the rain, and some surfaces can become slippery.
■ It is easy to settle for what your local retailer holds, but try to shop around – the range of materials generally available is now extremely large.

△ **TEXTURED PAVING**
Textured slabs provide an inexpensive and convenient alternative to small units.

▽▷ **SMALL UNIT PAVING**
Small pavers create a richly textured look and make paving awkward areas relatively easy, but they are more expensive to lay than larger paving slabs.

△ **INTERLOCKING PAVERS**

▽ **NATURAL STONE**
Its variable thickness makes natural stone difficult to lay, but it is always attractive.

△ **TERRACOTTA**

△ **GRANITE PAVERS**

50 THE BENEFITS OF GRAVEL SURFACES

Gravel or shingle is suitable for just about any location in the yard.

• Gravel is cheaper and easier to lay than hard surfacing materials such as concrete, stone, or brickwork.

• Many plants will grow through gravel if it is not more than 4 in (10 cm) in depth. Planting in areas of gravel rather than in specific beds of soil creates a random, relaxed look.

• Gravel is useful for brightening up basements or cellar areas, or for surfacing a flat rooftop.

△ A HARMONIOUS SETTING
Gravel chips of the same stone used in the wall and edgings provide a harmonious setting for the planting in this garden.

STONE-TYPE GRAVEL

FINE COLORED GRAVEL

SHINGLE

△ GRAVEL PATH
Replenish the top layer of gravel each summer to keep it looking neat and fresh.

51 CHOOSING & USING GRAVEL

An enormous range of gravel is available, so select a variety that suits your home. For driveways, it is wise to choose larger chippings that will not be trapped in the treads of your car tires. Areas of gravel or shingle must always be properly contained (usually by edging tiles) to prevent chips spreading onto nearby beds and lawns. Rake the surface at regular intervals if you do not want plants to self-seed through the gravel. Although gravel is noisy to walk on, this can serve as a deterrent to intruders.

52 WOOD SURFACING

Decks are especially useful for creating a level outdoor space if your garden slopes dramatically. They also make an attractive surface in their own right and can be built with matching benches, planter boxes, and trellises.

▪ Decks become slippery in damp conditions. Use nonskid strips outside entranceways and on stairs to make safer.

△ DECKING PATHWAY
Here, a linear decking path is interrupted by a static circular design. Decking can be used as an alternative to paving, and gives a unified look when combined with fencing.

DECKING PATTERNS

53 SMALL LAWNS

Lawns can be beautiful to look at, but even the smallest lawn will require a considerable amount of work if it is to remain attractive. If you have children and pets, be sure to choose a hard-wearing grass for your area of lawn. For small areas taking no wear, consider using chamomile or low-growing thymes as planting for your lawn.

◁ A TIDY LAWN
A well-maintained lawn is a delight to look at and makes a good place to relax in the summer sunshine.

54 GROUNDCOVER

In a small garden, groundcover plants make an excellent alternative to grass, especially in odd-shaped areas. They can be used to link taller plants within a mixed planting design, or on their own to contrast with hard surfaces or gravel. For year-round cover choose an evergreen, such as ground ivy (*Glechoma hederacea*).

- Groundcover plants are ideal for suppressing weeds. However, be sure to contain those plants described as rampant or invasive or you may be forced to spend as much time keeping them under control as you would spend pulling up weeds.

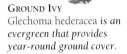

GROUND IVY
Glechoma hederacea *is an evergreen that provides year-round ground cover.*

GROUNDCOVER CHOICE
Ajuga reptans
Anthemis cupaniana
Armeria maritima
Caltha palustris
Euonymus fortunei
Festuca glauca
Lamium maculatum
Lavandula
Polygonum bistorta
Saponaria ocymoides
Stachys lanata
Thymus

GROUNDCOVER PLANTING DESIGN
In this garden design, ground-cover plants provide year-round interest with flower color, texture and leaf shape.

Stepping stones help keep plant masses separate and allow access for gardener

This creeping rose, Rosa 'Nozomi', has pink and white flowers

Antique border pinks, Dianthus, have masses of fragrant flowers

Lamb's ears (Stachys lanata) has charming, woolly gray foliage

PLANNING YOUR PLANTING

55 STRUCTURAL PLANTING

STRUCTURED DESIGN

Once the hard structure of your yard is in place, bring it to life with planting. For a harmonious effect in a small garden, it is crucial to consider your planting as a whole.
- Choose planting material that is in scale with the layout and features of your yard.
- Consider the composition of each grouping of plants; plant in masses rather than singles.
- Opt for distinctive shapes, forms, textures, or fragrances to provide year-round interest.

56 FEATURE PLANTS

When planning your yard, first decide what your feature plants, or "specials," are going to be. These can be used as a visual link between your planting and the surrounding architecture, for instance a weeping cherry, *Prunus*, curving over a pool wall. On a much smaller scale, your "special" planting might be a yucca acting as an evergreen pivot among a group of perennials.

DECIDUOUS FEATURE PLANT ▷
This hydrangea provides a glorious focal point. Use a pot to change the character of feature plants that are past their peak.

57 SKELETON PLANTS

Once you have chosen your feature plants, select species that will establish the year-round structure of your yard. As a guideline, go for plants that look good in winter: evergreen plants that will be eclipsed in summer by attention-seeking shrubs, but which come into their own in winter either for their form or foliage. Ivy is particularly useful for small gardens, as are euonymus and cotoneasters. Grow bay and boxwood as clipped container plants. Within borders, smaller evergreens and shrubby herbs such as spirea can be used as a backdrop.

△ SPRING
The boxwood acts as a backdrop to the lime green flower heads of euphorbia.

△ SUMMER
In summer the euphorbia changes color and many annuals appear.

△ AUTUMN
The euphorbias have been deadheaded, asters now provide the color.

58 SEASONAL INTEREST

Having selected your skeleton plants, choose your seasonal decorative shrubs. In small yards, shrubs that perform well over two or three seasons provide the best value. Group shrubs to keep them in scale with the design of your garden; the width of the terrace they border, for instance. Avoid using too many single specimens since they may compete with the feature plants.

◁ A SEASONAL SPRAY
This Helictotrichon produces a spray of flowers from May to June, when it is engulfed in white dianthus and foxgloves.

59 DECORATIVE PLANTING

Once the framework of your planting has been established, then choose annuals and biennials to fill in any gaps while you wait for your long-term planting to become established. Annuals can be found in an enormous variety of colors and habits, so select your plants carefully to suit the site and color plan. Sunflowers, for example, are annuals that grow to over 10 ft (3 m) tall, making ideal fillers at the back of a sunny border. Fast-growing climbers such as hops can fullfill the same function. For quick fillers at a lower level, you might choose calendulas, nasturtiums, or forget-me-nots.

△ COMBINED COLOR
Campanulas and orange rock roses, Helianthemum, *combine well.*

▽ ANNUAL BORDER
Annuals grow in a vast range of colors and forms; a species can be found to fill any part of a border.

SEASONAL FILL-IN ▷
A species of pansy, Viola, *can be found to come into flower in every season, so it is an excellent filler.*

60 THE BEAUTY OF BULBS

Bulbous plants are particularly useful in a small yard because they can be lifted out of the ground after their flowering period and stored away until the following year – allowing space for other flowers to take their place. Bulbs are ideal for window boxes; they can be planted in layers below other plants, making the most of the limited space. Their upright form provides a pleasing contrast to trailing plants. Many bulbs, such as the narcissus shown here, are ideal for cutting, and a vase of cut flowers taken from the yard is a perfect way of creating a link between inside and out (*see p.10*).

△ *NARCISSUS*
'GRAND SOLEIL D'OR'

▽ CONTRASTING MASSES
Spring-flowering bulbs,
such as these yellow lily-
flowered tulips and grape
hyacinths, are ideal for
planting en masse.

61 COLOR IN YOUR YARD

Choose plants that combine to create a harmonious color composition, as opposed to a strongly contrasting one, to give your garden a sense of unity and, as a result, a greater sense of space. Be aware of the effect color has on the mood of your yard.

- Yellow and gold are warm, sunny colors that will brighten any area.
- Varying shades of purple combine well with deep greens and bronzes to provide a somber, mysterious air.
- Choose plants with gray and silver foliage to create a light, airy feel.

△ A MEDLEY OF HUES
Cottage gardens are characterized by their random mixtures of color. Note how reds dominate other colors.

62 SCENTED GARDEN

Small yards really come into their own when planted for fragrance. The smaller your space, the closer to your scented plants you will be; the more enclosed your space, the more intense their perfume. To enjoy the scent of flowers, both outside and in your home, plant fragrant roses around your windows and aromatic herbs in a tub by your kitchen door. Grow fragrant lilies and hyacinths in containers on the patio, or cut them and fill your home with perfume.

△ HEAVENLY SCENT
Damask roses have a heady fragrance. These old-fashioned roses are popular favorites for country-style gardens.

◁ SCENTED SHRUB
Viburnum x burkwoodii *has sweet-scented flowers.*

47

PLANTING ENVIRONMENTS

63 ANALYZING YOUR ENVIRONMENT

Assess your site so that you are aware which areas of the garden are most suitable for which species of plants. How well, if at all, plants thrive in your yard will depend on a number of factors:

■ How much sun reaches your site? Note the direction of the sun at noon in relation to your house, and observe also where shade is cast by boundary fences, trees, and so on.

■ Winds and drafts can render a yard unusable, so check which direction winds are coming from.

■ Analyze your soil. Is it an acid or an alkaline soil? Is it waterlogged or dry? These factors will dictate which plants will grow successfully.

SITE ASSESSMENT ▷
This garden is exposed to sun for long periods but the solid fence gives an area of shade.

Hardy rose tolerates drafty site

Ivy grows up shady wall

Container plants grown on patio area

Raised bed for rock plants

64 SUN-LOVING PLANTS

Most plants love sunshine, and the real sun-lovers – snapdragons, dahlias, geraniums, and gladioli, to mention a handful – produce the most strikingly colorful flowers. The majority of fruits and roses thrive in full sun. For areas of intense sunshine that are prone to droughts, cacti and succulents, palms, and yuccas will survive even baking conditions. Generally, look for species that are naturally conditioned for survival in hot, sunny climates. Most Mediterranean plants will thrive.

△ DAHLIA

△ MORNING GLORY
A fast-growing annual, Convolvulus tricolor 'Blue Flash' displays its intense blue flowers in summer.

PLANTS THAT THRIVE IN FULL SUNSHINE

Agapanthus	Geranium	Rosmarinus
Buddleia davidii	Hebe	Salvia
Cistus	Iris x germanica	Stachys byzantina
Cortaderia	Lavandula	Tamarix hispida
Dianthus	Papaver orientale	Viola hederacea

65 SEMISHADE PLANTS

Although the majority of plants require the maximum amount of light to achieve their optimum growth, not all plants will tolerate strong direct sunlight, and many species prefer to grow in a shaded area. Plants that enjoy light shade include the fragrant honeysuckle and the ever-popular fuchsia. In general, look for plants that are naturally acclimatized to woodland conditions, such as hydrangeas, lilies, and azaleas.

△ HONEYSUCKLE
An attractive and fragrant climbing plant, honeysuckle brings perfume and color to shady locations.

PLANTS THAT THRIVE IN SEMISHADE

Aucuba	Helleborus	Nicotiana
Bergenia	Impatiens	Polygonum
Buxus	Lilium	Skimmia
Convallaria	Muscari	Vinca
Cyclamen	Myosotis	Viola

49

66 DRY SHADE PLANTING

Many plants that enjoy sunshine will nevertheless tolerate shady conditions if the soil remains suitably dry. These plants, which include many colorful species, such as *Liriope muscari*, can do much to brighten dull sites. However, the majority of plants that actually enjoy shady conditions are usually chosen for the texture, shape, or sheen of their foliage.

△ **LILYTURF**
Liriope muscari is an evergreen perennial that will tolerate dry shade. Its spikes of lavender flowers appear in the autumn.

PLANTS SUITABLE FOR DRY SHADE		
Ajuga	Lamium	Ruscus aculeatus
Bergenia	Lonicera pileata	Sambucus
Cotoneaster	Lunaria	Skimmia japonica
Cyclamen coum	Osmanthus	Tellima
Hedera helix	Polygonatum	Vinca major
Ilex	Pulmonaria	Viola labradorica

67 DAMP SHADE PLANTING

Some of the hardier species of plant that ideally prefer sunshine will tolerate shady conditions as long as soil is sufficiently moist. Willow gentian, *Gentiana asclepiadea*, is a perennial with sprays of rich blue, late-summer flowers that can bring color to a damp shady area. Other favorites for damp shady conditions include marsh marigold, *Caltha palustris*; toad lily, *Tricyrtis formosana*; wake robin, *Trillium grandiflorum*; and *Jeffersonia dubia*.

WILLOW GENTIAN ▽

PLANTS SUITABLE FOR DAMP SHADE		
Aruncus dioicus	Hamamelis	Lythrum
Astilbe	Hedera colchica	Pieris
Aucuba japonica	Helleborus	Rheum palmatum
Camellia	Hosta	Sambucus
Cornus	Hydrangea	Viburnum davidii
Fatsia japonica	Ligustrum	Viburnum opulus

68 EXPOSED SITES

Grow tough shrubs, such as barberries, to shelter less hardy plants in exposed areas. If this is not possible, look for resilient plants, such as African daisy (*Osteospermum jucundum*). Tough grasses and heathers can be combined effectively, their massed forms provide a sculptural quality. Low-growing herbs, such as thyme, are hardy plants; succulents, such as hens-and-chickens, are useful for ground cover in exposed sites; and strap-leaved plants such as yuccas will also grow successfully. As a guide, look for plants that grow naturally in coastal areas, where conditions are harsh.

EXPOSED SITE CHOICE
Berberis
Centranthus ruber
Cistus
Cytisus
Daphne
Erica
Gaultheria procumbens
Genista lydia
Juniperus horizontalis
Lavandula
Philadelphus
Rosmarinus
Spartium junceum
Syringa patula
Ulex europaeus
Viburnum davidii

◁ AFRICAN DAISY

△ OX-EYE DAISY
A resilient and attractive carpet-forming species, Chrysanthemum leucanthemum *bears a mass of flowers in early summer.*

△ SEA HOLLY
An upright plant adapted to harsh coastal conditions, Eryngium x oliverianum *bears striking lavender-blue flowers.*

POTS & CONTAINERS

69 PRACTICAL POTS

Containers really come into their own in the small-space yard, since they make it possible to grow plants of any size in almost any location. They provide a practical way of decorating roofs, walls, decks, balconies, basements, and windows, as well as the more usual ground levels.
- Position pots to punctuate the layout of your small yard and as a means of introducing planting into any confined or awkward spaces.

POTTED ROSE
Pots can bring color and fragrance to paved areas of your small yard.

70 POTS OF STYLE

Choose pots carefully. Think about how the color, shape, and scale of your container will relate to the style and scale of your space.
- Half barrels, found at many garden centers, suit most situations.
- Terracotta containers should be frost-proof and simple in outline.
- Baskets make excellent short-term containers when lined with plastic, and can look charming when they are filled with sun-loving flowers.

◁ STUDIO POTS

WILLOW BASKETS, ▷
NATURAL OR PAINTED

▽ WOODEN BARREL

71 USING POTS WITHOUT PLANTING

When choosing a container, ask yourself whether you want the pot, trough, or tub to be the main focal point rather than the plants. A lovely oil jar, for instance, can be used without planting, providing pleasure in its shape and its contrast to the froth of surrounding plants.

72 PLANTS IN POTS

Just about any plant – herbs, vegetables, or small trees – can be grown in a container, provided it is given sufficient root space and is adequately watered and fed.

- Select a pot that complements the planting grown in it. As a rule of thumb, a plant should never be more than twice as tall as its pot.
- Consider color harmony – do you want a dramatic contrast or a subtle combination.
- Revitalize your established potted plants by replacing the top layer of soil mix each spring.

STANDARD CHRYSANTHEMUM ▷
Plants grown as standards, such as this chrysanthemum, look particularly attractive when grown in pots. The trailing plant at its base is stonecrop, Sedum.

73 POTTED HERBS

All shrubby herbs make good container plants. Place a pot of mixed herbs next to your kitchen door or beneath the window – as well as being convenient for culinary use, it will also be decorative and pleasantly fragrant.

- A strawberry pot is suitable for planting a mixture of herbs. Flowering chives, *Allium*, winter savory (*Satureja montana*), and shrubby thymes, *Thymus*, are useful, decorative herbs.
- Larger plants such as bay are particularly attractive grown as single specimens in pots.
- Mint should always be potted – it is invasive.

△ STRAWBERRY POT
PLANTED WITH HERBS

74 POTTED TREES

A tree planted in a container will provide long-term sculptural interest in your small yard. Where space permits, display tender trees, such as *Citrus* (which can make ideal container plants), on the patio in summer and bring them indoors over the winter months.

- Trees that are grown in pots will limit the height and spread of their growth to compensate for the confined root space.
- Revitalize your potted tree by replacing the top layer of soil mix each spring, and repot completely every three to five years.

△ LEMON TREE
A lemon tree grown in a pot makes a stylish feature for a patio space in a Mediterranean-style yard.

75 ARRANGING POTS

Groups of containers may not be significant in a larger yard, but they can be very effective in a smaller yard or on roof terraces, decks, and balconies. But take care when arranging your pots – a jumble of pots can look charming in the right environment, but a jumble can easily become a mess.

- Create a sense of decorative unity by arranging a group of similar pots, related in style and/or color.
- With more casual arrangements, the choice of plants should be formal enough to prevent the effect looking messy.

▽ STYLISH ARRANGEMENT
Grow plants in pots of a similar style to emphasize the plants' foliage and flowers.

76 USING CONTAINERS IN EXPOSED SITES

Plastic containers are useful for exposed sites such as rooftops and balconies. They are lighter than the natural materials they so often imitate, and they retain moisture.

A layer of pea gravel or pebbles on top of the soil mix will help retain moisture and prevent the soil from drying up and blowing away. It can also look attractive and deter weeds.

77 IMPROVISED POTS

Almost any kind of container possessing adequate drainage holes can be used for planting. In the Mediterranean and in Mexico all sorts of cans, pots, and pans are colorfully planted and massed together, bringing color and interest to doorways, alleyways, and courtyards. There is plenty of opportunity for inventive use of teapots, watering cans, wheelbarrows, plastic containers, and old sinks.

◁ DELIGHTFUL DISCARDS
"One-of-a-kind" containers have become so popular as improvised pots that many are available built in ceramic materials and sold in garden centers just for planting.

78 HANGING BASKETS

A hanging basket creates a charming miniature garden in itself that comes into its own when the only outdoor space available is a wall or a doorway. When choosing plants for hanging baskets or any containers positioned high on a wall, select plants that look good when seen from below or from the side. Most suitable are those whose stems meander gracefully, such as *Ballota*, or arch elegantly, such as Boston fern (*Nephrolepis exaltata*).
■ Line your hanging baskets with moss or a man-made porous material, and use a good-quality soil mix that will retain moisture.

GOLD COLOR SCHEME

FURNISHING FACTS

79 LIGHTING

Extend the enjoyment of your small yard by including some form of lighting in your design. It will enable you to read, eat, or simply sit around outside on warm spring and autumn evenings. If you can see your garden from indoors, it will enable you to enjoy a nighttime view of it throughout the year. Select spotlights to illuminate a statue or a group of pots, a courtesy lamp by your door to welcome guests, or a dazzling security light to deter unwelcome visitors.

△ ATMOSPHERIC LIGHTING
Subtle lighting creates a gentle glow beneath a specimen tree.

◁ LOW LIGHTING
Path lights provide ideal low-level illumination in gardens.

80 AWNINGS & FABRIC

Give your yard a sense of luxury by furnishing it with colorful covers, cushions, and umbrellas that will compensate for a lack of planting and create an inviting roomlike ambience. Consider using an awning to create a ceiling for your "room." It can provide shade or conceal a gray sky. It provides privacy if your garden is overlooked by neighbors.

◁ COLORFUL FABRICS
Fabrics for outside should be tough (and preferably washable) and suit the style of your garden space.

81 DUAL-PURPOSE FURNITURE

Build furniture to avoid the clutter often created by free-standing chairs and tables (and the problem of storing them in winter). Modify existing features to make seating space, or design new ones so that they serve a dual purpose.

Raise a wall around an existing pool, for example, to provide an area on which to sit, or build retaining walls at a suitable height for casual seating. Use a raised brick or concrete slab as a low table, or build a hollow brick bench for extra storage space.

WOODEN BENCH WITH LIFT-UP LID FOR STORAGE

82 INTEGRATE YOUR FURNISHINGS

Construct built-in furniture from a material that blends in with the rest of your garden. This gives your small garden a unified look that makes it appear larger. If using wood, always choose a hardwood, because softwoods tend to splinter.

Concrete is cheap and durable, but austere. Soften its appearance with trailing plants, or by combining it with another material such as wood. Brick is one of the best materials – its small unit size makes it possible to build furniture in awkward sites.

83 FREE-STANDING FURNITURE

When space is limited, you must take furniture into account at the earliest planning stage. Even the smallest free-standing table with a chair on either side needs a minimum 6 ft (2 m) of clear space – a considerable amount in a small site. Outdoor furniture should not appear as ill-considered clutter; its style must complement that of the house and garden.

■ Permanent furniture should have a settled look and a bulk that is in scale with its surroundings. Often the best way of achieving this is by having built-in furniture.

■ Make sure that a terrace where furniture is arranged temporarily for summer does not look neglected in winter. Try to visualize how your garden space will look without, as well as with, furniture.

EATING OUT ▷
This well-designed picnic table is sturdy, but many lightweight versions will not stand regular use.

STOWAWAY FURNITURE ▷
Ideal when storage space is limited, this style of furniture is designed to fold flat.

◁ STYLISH FURNISHING
Elegant, wrought-iron furniture such as this is perhaps best suited to a more formal-style garden.

84 TAKING ADVANTAGE OF TREES

Trees usually occupy a large proportion of the space in a small yard. Take maximum advantage of them by using them to save space at ground level. Trees make effective supports for hammocks or swings, for example. They also make ideal supports for lighting, which will illuminate the tracery of branches. Trees provide shade during hot weather, so the base of a tree is the perfect spot for an attractive bench.

UNDER THE APPLE TREE
A white-painted wooden bench makes a practical and attractive feature.

85 COORDINATING STYLES

It is worth investing in a beautifully designed and constructed table or chair to link the interior and exterior of your house. The visual connection between the indoor and outdoor space is particularly important with small sites (*see p.10*).

Soften the division between inside and out by having outdoor furniture that complements the style of your indoor furniture, or by linking the color of the upholstery. Arrange your outdoor furniture so that it looks good from indoors also.

ILLUSIONS OF GRANDEUR

86 THINKING BIG

Avoid cluttering your small space with a collection of miniature objects. As the art of the interior decorator shows, the fewer the number of objects in a small room and the simpler the range of colors and fabrics, the larger it will appear. Apply these principles to your outdoor space to create the same effect. Limit the number of objects in your yard, and scale them up, rather than down. Try to stick to a simple range of materials, matching existing structures.

ONE FOR THE POT ▷
The dramatic shape of a single terracotta pot is usually preferable to the clutter that is created by a collection of small pots.

87 *TROMPE L'OEIL* EFFECTS

There are a number of design tricks and techniques that can be exploited to decorate your yard in a theatrical or dramatic way using paint, trellis, mirrors, or light. These devices can often create the illusion of size in the smallest of areas. Such techniques, referred to collectively as *trompe l'oeil* effects, are especially compatible with the style of man-made surroundings and can provide inventive ways of decorating damp, shady spaces where conditions are too inhospitable for plants to grow.

88 DECEPTIVE PERSPECTIVE

Exploit the effect of natural perspective – where distant objects appear to be smaller than nearby objects of the same size – to give your garden the illusion of length.

▪ Place tall plants in the foreground, and grade down to shorter ones toward the end of the garden.

▪ Achieve the same effect with pots, which, ideally, should be identical in every way apart from their size.

▪ Make paths taper as they extend down the length of your yard.

▪ Grade a boundary fence or hedge so that it gradually shortens toward the end of your yard.

Here, all four trees are the same height

UP THE GARDEN PATH
Although these plots are the same size, the one on the right seems longer due to distorted perspective.

Shortest trees at end of site

Large pot placed in foreground

89 TRELLISWORK TRICKERY

Even if your only outlook is a wall, you can still create spectacular effects and spatial illusions using trelliswork designs to manipulate the natural laws of perspective (*see above*). Try painting the wall behind the trellis in a pale recessive color to emphasize the sense of depth (sky blue and other pale colors will give the impression of distance, while bright red and other bold colors appear to leap forward toward the viewer).

AN ILLUSION OF SPACE ▷
The design of this trelliswork gives the illusion of depth on a flat surface. Note that some of the slats are tapered.

90 PAINTED ILLUSIONS

An abstract mural or painted *trompe l'oeil* can bring vitality to the darkest of walls.

- Paint a doorway to suggest another garden lying beyond your own, or a window with a window box (the window box could be real).
- Paint plants where real ones cannot grow or to supplement the existing vegetation.
- Use exterior-grade paint on your garden wall. Different effects can be achieved using matte or eggshell finishes or by using bold stencils and spray paint to create patterns.
- If paint is your medium you can afford to be bold in your design, because mistakes can be painted over and a fresh start can be made.

△ PAINTED PIGEONS
A charming mural like this can be created even in the smallest and darkest sites.

91 MAGICAL MIRRORS

Strategically positioned mirrors can be employed to reflect the space that you already have and visually double the size of your yard.

- A mirror placed in a doorway, or a bricked-up archway, can give the impression of being an entrance to an area of yard beyond your own.
- Use a mirror as a screen to obscure an unwanted view in your yard.
- Large areas of mirror can brighten shady sites and subground areas.
- Always use mirrors at least ¼ in (6 mm) thick. Remember that they must be spotless to be effective.

◁ DOUBLE TAKE
A huge mirror has been positioned on a wall glimpsed through a decorative archway, giving the illusion of a second arch beyond.

92 A TRICK OF LIGHT & SHADE

In areas where natural light is intense, position plants or strong architectural features where they will cast dramatic shadows on the surrounding surfaces. If the light is not intense enough to produce well-defined shadows, paint some. Use a range of tones of the same color to imitate shadows of varying intensity.

- Increase the amount of sunlight reaching planting in shady areas by using mirrors or water features to reflect light toward the area. But do not put mirrors in bright positions: reflected light may singe plants.
- Let more light into your garden by replacing a solid fence with an open one to increase the apparent space.

△ LIGHT FEATURE
A "window" cut in a hedge creates an unusual focal point in this small garden.

◁ NATURAL SHADOW
Pergola horizontals create exciting shadows in this sunny Mediterranean site.

93 WORKING WITH WATER

However shallow, a pool of water will always make your space appear larger than it actually is.
- Use light-absorbent lining, such as black butyl rubber, to make the surface reflect surroundings.
- Alternatively, use light-reflecting lining (mirror tiles for example) to

reflect overhanging features, such as a piece of sculpture or some eye-catching plants, and to increase the amount of light in your garden.
- A mirror placed alongside water will increase visual excitement and give your space the appearance of added light and size.

A SUITABLE STYLE

94 COUNTRY-STYLE GARDEN

Understanding the essence of a style is the key to interpreting it in your own small space. The classic cottage-style garden has a homey rural image of roses rambling around a door, rough stone walls or split-rail fencing, and abundant planting.

- Choose unsophisticated plants – daisylike flowers, such as chrysanthemums and asters; calendulas; sweet peas; and hollyhocks.
- Natural materials are the obvious choice for outdoor furniture; use anything and everything for containers. Simple clay pots are suitably unsophisticated.

△ COUNTRY FLOWERS
Old-fashioned flowers such as delphiniums, sweet peas, and alliums still form the essence of the cottage-garden look.

◁ COUNTRY-STYLE COLOR
The clean lines of a simple terracotta pot contrast well with the masses of silvery artemisia and blue Nepeta mussinii.

△ FORMAL FLOWER BEDS
*Here, the planting is limited so
as not to lessen the impact of
the overall design.*

95 FORMAL GARDEN

The key to a formal garden style is in symmetry and order, characterized by neatly clipped hedges, elegant statuary, straight paths, and closely mown lawns. Such gardens need regular maintenance, for minor flaws tend to leap out from such precisely balanced design.
■ A carefully chosen point of focus, such as an elegant, unplanted oil jar will strike the right note of sophistication. A formal pool might be included to reflect the overall symmetry.
■ Echo a symmetrical layout with molded terracotta tubs planted with clipped boxwood.

96 MODERN GARDEN

Simplicity of line and a strong sense of space are characteristics of the modern-style garden. Function takes precedence, so plunge pools and hot tubs definitely fit the look.
■ Vegetation should be striking and architectural, so incorporate large-leaved hostas and spiky grasses.
■ Large concrete tubs can help create the modern look – terracotta works when the shapes are clean and bold.
■ Make comfort a top priority when choosing furniture. Modern designs, such as director's chairs, are a popular option.
■ Choose square tiles to divide up your space geometrically.

LESS IS MORE ▷
*Restraint is essential when
choosing accessories for your
modern-style garden.*

Large-leaved
hosta

97 COLONIAL STYLE

The essence of a colonial-style garden is homeyness and comfort. Position a hammock or rocking chair on a neat, wooden veranda to capture the relaxed, unhurried mood. Rose-covered arbors and boxwood hedging can provide an echo of gracious living, but choose simple materials. Statuary is unpretentious – figures of animals in stone or wood are perfect. White picket fencing has a clean, crisp, colonial look; paths can be laid with slate or simple wood chips.

△ RELAXED PLANTING
Planting is allowed to sprawl against the clapboard walls, but notice the gentle counterpoise of the rose standard.

▽ COLONIAL CONTAINERS
White-painted pots planted with herbs suggest a folksy simplicity that is the key to colonial-style gardening.

Avoid pretension or abstraction with statuary

Wood is the natural choice for furniture

98 MEDITERRANEAN-STYLE GARDEN

Vivacious colors are the key to a Mediterranean-style garden. Terracotta and ceramic pots should overflow with cascading flowers in vibrant reds, yellows, oranges, and blues against a backdrop of crisp white walls and spiky yucca plants. Create an area of terrace surfaced with stone or terracotta to provide a place to eat outdoors and entertain guests. Shade, therefore, is also a crucial element, and umbrellas or awnings – the bigger (and brighter) the better – strike the perfect note. Furniture, too, should be brightly colored – perhaps café-style. A lemon tree in a terracotta tub or a classical stone or ceramic statue provides the archetypal Mediterranean focal point.

△ **DECORATIVE FRUIT**
If you do not have the space to grow citrus trees in tubs, display the fruit in colorful bowls.

SUITABLE CERAMICS ▷
Simple terracotta tiles provide the appropriate surfacing material for a Mediterranean garden. Colorful glazed ceramic tiles look good on walls, complementing the natural vibrancy of sea and sky.

Use pebbles for decoration

The ubiquitous terracotta pot is ideal

Mosaic tiles

Yucca plant

99 ORIENTAL GARDEN

When creating an oriental-style garden you should aim to instill a mood of serene and contemplative calm into your design. Bamboo or brushwood is appropriate for fencing. Look for textural detailing when choosing containers.

■ Rocks and mossy stones are important styling details for their solid mass and sculptural shapes.

■ Stained decking and gravel (raked into swirling patterns for maximum effect) are suitable surfacing materials for an oriental-style garden.

■ Exploit the natural textures and rough shapes of rocks and driftwood to make seats and other furnishings. Always keep seating low.

△ PRACTICAL PAVING
Stone paving is practical if you do not want a gravel pattern to be disturbed.

▽ SERENE COLORS
A water feature adds to the sense of calm. Choose planting for its leaf texture. Colors should be serene.

100 COURTYARD GARDEN

A courtyard garden is an obvious choice for a small enclosed urban area. Patio surfacing, which typifies a courtyard garden, helps to provide a low-maintenance space that is ideal for practical outdoor living.

▪ Planting can still be enjoyed in containers and small raised beds. Indeed, plants are essential to soften the hard lines of walls and paving.

▪ Take advantage of vertical space by planting fragrant climbers, such as honeysuckle. Consider a potted tree to provide an area of shade.

△ FONT FEATURE
An old stone font makes an ideal focal point for this courtyard. Alchemilla mollis *softens the font's hard lines.*

△ INFORMAL POND
This small pond, teeming with golden carp, is ideally suited to its rural setting. Water lilies adorn the surface.

101 WATER GARDEN

Your choice of plant type is crucial when you are planning to establish a small pond.

▪ The smaller the surface area of the water, the more important it is to include oxygenating plants such as *Elodea canadensis* in your choice.

▪ Dwarf water lilies, *Nymphaea*, can be planted in water that is only 6 in (15 cm) deep, making them an ideal choice for small ponds.

▪ Decking is the best surfacing for water gardens; select furniture and fencing in a matching wood. A stone statue will enhance the look.

▪ Informal ponds can look idyllic in a rural location, but a more formal raised or sunken brick pond is better suited to an urban environment.

INDEX

ACKNOWLEDGMENTS

DK would like to thank Hilary Bird for
compiling the index, Isobel Holland for proofreading, Fiona Wild
for editorial assistance, Murdo Culver for design assistance, and
Mark Bracey for computer assistance.

Photography

KEY: t *top*; b *bottom*; c *center*; l *left*; r *right*

All photographs by Geoff Dann and Steve Wooster except;
Peter Anderson 3, 11l, 52t, 53b; Clive Boursell 4; John Brookes 62t;
Boys Syndication 10l; Linda Burgess (**Garden Picture Library**)
61b; Eric Crichton 50b, 51t; Robert Estall (**Garden Picture
Library**) 33br; Neil Fletcher 46t, 49b, 49t; John Glover 62b; Jerry
Harpur 51br; Stephen Hayward 66t; Jacqui Hurst 9bl, 13t, 14b,
18l, 20bl, 22l, 22r, 25mr, 28tr, 36l, 45t, 47bl, 65tl; Dave King 10r,
11tr, 11br, 26r, 34mr, 34bl, 58bl, 64tr, 65br, 66b,67; Andrew
Lawson 35br; Andrew de Lory 20tl; Damien Moore 14t, 17t, 19br,
25bl, 127t, 27b, 28br, 31tl, 41tr, 54, 68; Elvin McDonald 13b;
Howard Rice 50t; Tim Ridley 5, 23tr, 29, 38t, 41ml, 52b; Kim
Taylor 37b; Colin Walton 1, 19t, 42t; Matthew Ward 8, 9tl, 15,
43b, 53t, 55, 72b; **Elizabeth Whiting & Assoc**. 62l.

The designs on pages 8, 9, 15, 53, 55 originally appeared in
Container Gardening by Malcolm Hillier, Dorling Kindersley, 1991.

Illustrations

Martine Collings 37; Karen Cochrane 39; Liz Peperall 45;
Colin Salmon 48.